LET'S TALK MONEY

GET BUDGET RESULTS WITHOUT A BUDGET

BY ERIC HUDSON

This book may be purchased in bulk for educational, business, fund-raising, or sales promotional use. For book orders visit ohmyoils.com.

Published by McLean Essentials, LLC
Birmingham, AL 35242

ISBN 978-0-9983457-2-7

Printed In the United States of America.

To purchase copies of this book please visit ohmyoils.com.

V1/5-2017

Contents

Introduction
Acknowledgements 1
The Mission Of This Book 1
About Me 2
Preface 5

Chapter 1. Getting Started 7

Chapter 2. Holding Account 11

Chapter 3. Monthly Fixed 15

Chapter 4. Irregular Expenses 19

Chapter 5. Everyday Expenses 23

Chapter 6. His/Her Freedom 27

Chapter 7. The How To 29

Chapter 8. Emergency Fund 33

Chapter 9. Saving for the Future 35

Chapter 10. The Wrap Up 37

Acknowledgements

It's safe to say that a project like this doesn't get accomplished alone. I'm eternally grateful to my family for supporting and enduring me through this process. Vanessa and Savannah, you're the reason I live. This book couldn't have come together without the amazing design talents of Michael Durham. Thanks to Chase Brown, Tiffany Sommer, Joan McLean, Nicole Radmacher, Yvonne Ahart, Jeremie, Sandy, and Amanda Hudson for help with the proof reads and ideas. Thanks to the rest of the amazing McLean Team for their constant support. A big thank you to Jeremiah and Monique McLean for the opportunity and for pushing me to step out and do something like this. I would never have had the courage on my own. Finally, I would like to thank the Lord for His grace in my life. I am rescued daily because of Him.

The Mission Of This Book

I am sure you are like me. You want to do good things with the financial resources you've been given. The mission of this book is to teach you how to do those good things automatically. I will show you how to prioritize and schedule your financial life so your family's money goals and priorities are met every month, guaranteed. You will live at peace knowing your financial values and responsibilities are being funded each month without you even having to think about them. Then the fun begins, as you're allowed to enjoy what's left over guilt free, because the important things have already been paid. How can this happen? Well my friend, you'll have to read further...

About Me

To say I was born in a rural area is an understatement. Our house was surrounded on three sides by pastureland and on the back by a pond and woods. Our town didn't even have a red light. We weren't completely living in the dark ages, we did have a caution light. Boom!

I'm unaware of anyone in my family having ever earned a four-year college degree. During my high school years, college was never brought up in conversation within my family, at least that I can remember. I did end up attending a little technical college and received an Associate's Degree in Electronics Engineering.

The plan for almost everyone I knew was to graduate, find a job, get married, and move into a manufactured home on family land somewhere. In keeping with the culture, I proposed to and married my high school sweetheart Vanessa at 20 years of age. We didn't take the normal route and move to family land. We took what little education I had, and we moved to the big city of Birmingham, AL.

It is very popular in our culture today to encourage kids to find what they're passionate about and pursue those passions to find a suitable career. That was not the case where and when I grew up. What you were good at or what you liked never really came into the conversation. Your requirement, as a young man at least, was to find a job, work hard, and do whatever it took to provide for your family, even if you were miserable for 40 years. You were allowed to have fun at night or on the weekends, but work had only one purpose, and that was to provide for your family.

It wasn't until much later in life that I learned to pursue my passions. I began working for Brasfield & Gorrie in 2004 and the leadership there challenged me to do just that. They allowed me to become a Dave Ramsey counselor and begin to help people get out of debt, save, etc. My Director of Operations, Marty Hardin, encouraged me, and I'll forever be in his debt for helping me. During this time, I learned that I had a passion for understanding money, how it works, and how to help people reach their goals and gain peace in their financial lives.

After becoming a Dave Ramsey counselor, Vanessa and I really worked hard to follow his plan to the letter. I respect and admire Dave so much. I don't believe there has been anyone that has done more to help people get out of debt than Dave. Unfortunately, we realized we couldn't stick with budgeting and the cash envelope system. We could do it for a while, but then we would fall back into bad habits. It was frustrating because we really wanted to do it. I understood how important it was, but we just couldn't seem to pull it off. Here I am, an official Dave Ramsey counselor, and although we didn't go back into debt, we could not use his system to manage our finances day to day, week to week, and month to month. It was defeating, embarrassing and frustrating.

Somewhere around this time I read a book called "The Automatic Millionaire" by David Bach. The premise of this book was that you could become wealthy if you simply "paid yourself first." The magic of it was to pay yourself first automatically. Now what does it mean to pay yourself first? The way most of us approach saving money is we tell ourselves that at the end of the month, if there's any money left after we've paid our bills, we will save that money. The problem is, there's never any money left. Something always happens, or we always find somewhere to spend the money.

The premise of "The Automatic Millionaire" was to decide how much you want to save each month, whether that be a percentage or a fixed amount and have that come out of your check before anything else. Then, have those dollars deposited into a retirement or investment account. In other words, pay yourself first. Additionally, the transfer should happen automatically. Then adjust your lifestyle to live off what is left.

Bach's idea made total sense to me. It also sparked an idea of my own. What if you could automate all or almost all your financial decisions? What if you could predetermine where your money went before you got your hands on it? Could this happen, and could this idea work? This idea would not have worked when Vanessa and I were first married in 1990. There wasn't any such thing as mobile banking. But in 2005, this looked like it could be a real possibility. So, I decided to try it. I decided I would try to take Dave Ramsey's cash envelope system and automate it, using multiple accounts and debit cards. The reason you're reading this book today is because it worked! Admittedly, it was a little rough and clumsy at first, but now, I wouldn't live any other way. And, here's the good news. I'm going to show you how to do it, step-by-step. Are you ready? Let's change your life!

Preface

Before we get started, I feel I should stop here and give a piece of advice to those of you who have a home-based business or business of any kind. You should have a business-only bank account for business-only transactions. Your salary that you pull from that business account is a business expense, but when you turn around and deposit your salary into your personal account, it becomes your family's income. You should never pay for personal expenses with money from your business account. Transfer money from your business account into your personal account first and then pay your bills from that account.

Here's an example. Let's say you need to go grocery shopping, but you don't have enough money in your personal account to make the purchase. You will need to pull the money from your business account as salary (business expense) and deposit it into your personal account (family income). Now you use the money from your personal account to purchase the groceries. It's best to do it this way because you can take a deduction for business expenses at tax time. If you don't have a business account or if you've muddied the business account by using it for personal expenses, then it becomes challenging to remember which expense was business related and which was personal. This could cost you money by either overpaying your tax bill, because you didn't count all your legitimate business expenses, or if you count things as business expenses that aren't, you could end up on the wrong side of an audit. Just trust me and keep them separate.

Chapter 1

GETTING STARTED

First Things First

First off, if you are married or if you are sharing income and expenses with someone in your household, this system works best when there is agreement. If you alone make the decision and you don't have your significant other on board, this system will not work like it should. I think it's important enough to bribe, beg, plead, do whatever you must do to get your partner to watch my videos on finances (ohmyoils.com/videos/money) or read this book to get an understanding of what you're wanting to do. See if you can get to common ground. Ask them if they agree that as a team you could be doing better with money by saving more, giving more, paying off debt, etc. If you can get a "yes" answer to that question, then explain that what you're wanting to set up is the easiest, most workable system in the whole wide world.

> **"Working this plan with your partner is imperative to your success."**

Committing to this system does take a little planning, but after that, it really runs itself. Not only that, every month there will be guilt-free money in your accounts to do with whatever you want, no questions asked and no judgement. As a matter of fact, you and your significant other will cheer each other on no matter how they spend the money.

Second, you will be opening several savings/checking accounts at your bank. This system works best when all accounts are at the same bank. These accounts should be free, allow unlimited transactions (on the checking accounts), have low or no minimum balance requirements, and provide electronic access.

If you haven't yet printed out my Easy Financial Flowchart, go ahead and do that now. It can be found at ohmyoils.com/videos/money. It is a free download. Print that out, and we'll use it to walk through the program. Don't worry if the flowchart and boxes don't make sense to you yet, they will as you read through the book.

At the end of this book, I will walk through opening the accounts with your bank. The reason I'm not having you do that now is because this plan is customizable to your financial situation. I want you to read this book and work the program, but I want you to work in the spirit of the book and not necessarily do it exactly the way I do it. Make it yours. This plan is designed to create peace in your life, not another set of dogmatic rules for you to follow.

Ok, let's take a look at the Flowchart.

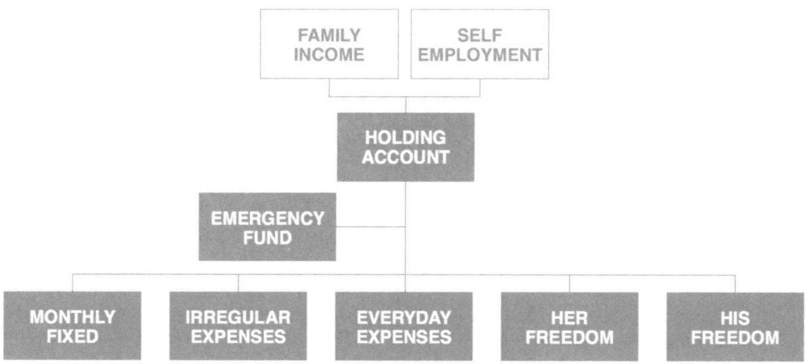

White Boxes - Family Income/Self Employment Salary

What qualifies as family income and self-employment salary? What I mean by this is all the streams of income from all the jobs you and your partner have that are for your personal use/expenses. I'm specific here because the way we're going to use this system is for home use. For those of you that have a home-based business or are self-employed, your income would not be the gross amount your business makes each month. Your income would be what you have decided to pull out of that business as a salary.

provider side of operational use, while users are represented as agents, and their behaviour is modelled in their sections in the chapters on tasks and communication.

In our breakdown, we identified several areas of legal interest. Of essential legal importance are the task, agent and communication chapters in the design theme. These are the areas that accommodate compliance engineering. Compliance engineering constitutes the regulating architecture in the sense of Lessig's (o.c.) 'code as law'. We now focus on compliance engineering in the El Cheapo case.

Earlier, in your capacity as an advisor of the CEO of De Telegraaf, you told him that difficulties may arise when the El Cheapo service under construction will use publicly available data from data bases that may nonetheless be protected by law. Several threats have to be faced, you mention. The data in these databases may be protected by copyright on its own merits; using the data may pass by the advertisements on the home page of the databases, resulting in damages; trademarks may be passed by in a similar manner; the structure of the database may be protected by copyright; substantial sums of money may have been invested in acquisition, management or presentation of the data, resulting in database law protection. The CEO asks you to provide risk assessments of all these threats with respect to the NVM service. You find that the copyright threats are nonexistent since there is no personal connection between the presentation of information on the houses for sale and the maker of these presentations – hardly any individual choice is made. You find that passing by the home page of the public service will hardly be a risk, if it is performed in a manner that does not violate database protection since then it will be almost identical to the issue of deep linking,[34] provided that El Cheapo generates a list of available houses and uses the technique of deep linking for providing further data on individual houses. Consequently, the important questions concern whether substantial sums of money have been invested in acquisition, management or presentation of the data in the NVM service and whether the El Cheapo use of the NVM database constitutes substantial use of the database. The first question seems easy and factual. First-instance judge Du Pon states the following:

> ... Set aside that generally speaking it is highly probable that the maintenance of a countrywide collection of 45,000 records that – considering their short-lived reliability – must be updated daily in order to keep them up-to-date continually will require a quantitative substantial investment,...

and your advice that, knowing these facts, your insistence on the substantial-investment criterion being fulfilled is reasonable – we further leave the issue alone.[35] More to the point is the additional criterion of substantial use of the database. Reviewing the **kranten.com** case mentioned earlier, you will advise making use of the public NVM service in the following manner: let the search agent come up with a list of addresses and prices of the relevant houses for sale, integrate the list with the list based

34 A question decided upon in the **kranten.com** case by the Rotterdam court in a summary decision of 22-08-2000, LJN-nummer: AA6826 Zaaknr: 139609/KG ZA 00-846 (in Dutch)

35 This notwithstanding the Appeal Court's decision denying this reading of the substantial-investment criterion – which, by the way, was reversed again by the Supreme Court. Anyway, this criterion is not of interest for the compliance engineering issue, since it is not directed towards efficient, but towards compliant IT design..

on the relevant houses from De Telegraaf's own housing special and other lists from other sources, and make additional information available through deep linking. In this operational model, you will run only a small risk of a successful NVM claim against De Telegraaf based on database protection right infringement. This is an example of what we consider to be compliance engineering. To do so, you need to understand the tasks, agent and communication chapters of the contextual model at the design-theme level.

In the El Cheapo case the following happened. In the first instance judge Du Pon said:

> ... According to Article 1, Section 1, under c, of the Database Act, 'use request' is understood to mean: the permanent or temporary transport of the contents of a database or a part of it onto another medium, irrespective of method and format employed. In our summary judgment, what El Cheapo does after a visitor of its site has made a search request is inside this definition. For it has been established that El Cheapo in such a case does copy a selection of files of NVM's database, stores them on its own server and saves them there for some time. ...

Interestingly, the court's reading of what is going on after a use request on the El Cheapo server (as design description of the tasks performed) is so far beside the point, that the appeal court decided the wording had to be rephrased:

> ... The principal claim 3 includes that in the argument ... of the first-instance ruling the word 'file' has been incorrectly used to denote one single house. This claim is founded, but cannot lead to nullification of the ruling. In those arguments 'record' or 'file-element' will be read instead of 'file'...

This in itself is an argument for some IT-schooling in legal education. Anyway, nobody doubts or doubted that El Cheapo makes use of 'use requests' in the sense of the Database Act. More to the point is whether these use requests result in substantial use. Judge Du Pon handles the issue as follows

> ...The principal defence against NVM's claim that such a substantial use is indeed the case implies that El Cheapo does not decide on the extent of the use, but that it depends on the way the user specifies his conditions (general or specific). Thus, El Cheapo merely offers the possibility to the user, to make El Cheapo request a substantial part. ... This defence does not hold ... The president himself has established by experience that in such a case often at least 10 files [records] appear, predominantly from the NVM database. This must count as a substantial part of that database. It may be added that smaller amounts of requested and presented files [records] often in any case will be considered as a qualitative substantial part of NVM's database, taking into account the type of the data (houses for sale) and the interest that even a limited number of these data can have for a visitor who more specifically is looking for a particular house and therefore has formulated a limited request. ...

and informs us that substantial use must not be interpreted with the extent and interest of the selection, relative to extent and interest of the data collection in the database, but relative to extent and interest of the selection the requesting user needs.

In the appeal case, no further light was shed on the substantial use issue. And the supreme court redirected the case to the appeal court level, where it is hoped that a more satisfactory interpretation will be found. However, we will have to wait and see.

As an advisor, you do not yet know of these decisions. You start an open-context analysis of the relevant pieces in the design chapter, looking for the IT-reconstruction of a substantial use issue. You keep the Dutch Database Act from 1999 and EU Directive 99/6/EU in mind. The EU Directive mentions the prevention of free-riding duplicating services as an overall goal. According to the explanatory memorandum of the Dutch Act, the goal of the Database Act is to prevent damages to the investor in a database through its re-use; it states as a principle that the investor has to prove these damages in order to make his claim stick. Combining these with the El Cheapo design, you decide that there is a real risk here: the type of re-use by El Cheapo is precisely what the Directive and the Database Act aim to prevent. Looking at the way this aim is worded in the text of the Act, however, you find that presenting 10 out of the 45,000 records in the NVM database is hard to understand as a substantial selection. The legal literature does not provide consistent guidance on the issue. Finally, you are aware of the enormous impact any first legal decision on this issue will have on future e-commerce developments. Consequently, in your advice you will argue that there is a considerable risk of a court order to discontinue the service under development if one of the database providers challenges the re-use in court, because its operation may be in conflict with the goals of the Database Act; that, nonetheless, the wording of the Act may find small selections for re-use acceptable; that otherwise the financial risks are limited to proven damages through re-use.

From a legal engineering point of view, you will mention that it will not be possible to remodel the service into compliance with the goals of the EU Directive, without fitting in agreements with the providers of databases that are meant to be used. If De Telegraaf is accepting the risk of the service eventually being closed down by a court order, it may choose to accommodate the textual reading of 'substantial use' as relative to database size. This is easily done by limiting the list of results to be presented with full record information. Another approach would be to remodel the service into only supplying a list of deep links to the relevant records in the NVM web service to the user, for these links are themselves not records in the NVM database. From the legal engineering point of view, you could investigate whether remodelling the El Cheapo service to sort and manipulate the list of links before being presented to the user will be acceptable. Even this is not clear – manipulation of selection results does technically imply copying the selection to the El Cheapo back-end temporarily, and feeding it into the manipulation-agent may in itself be considered as re-use.

In fact, the service under investigation will have to be launched, if at all, facing genuine legal ambiguity (what is substantial use?) – even where the applicable rules are very young. Engineering legal compliance into the El Cheapo service boils down to a legal risk analysis of the e-commercial services on the Internet and (re)modelling the functional design towards an acceptable level of the legal risks to be faced. To perform this task professionally, a legal advisor must be able to read and understand the design chapters of the contextual model as well as relate them to legal issues. As a matter of fact, this may also be a prerequisite for judges that have to decide on controversial e-commerce practices in summary cases.

4 LAW AS CODE – CODE AS LAW: THE FUTURE OF E-COMMERCE

The substantial use clause has been formulated in the EU Directive and adopted by the Dutch legislator. The legislator has to take into account how e-commerce on cyberspace will prosper and suffer, with and without the rules he is making. He will have to foresee the ways e-commerce practice might grow, the ways judges will read the open-texture concepts in individual cases and the result of e-commerce practice complying with this reading. His task is a difficult one, if we can take the Kazaa and El Cheapo cases to be exemplary.

From the inherent-ambiguity perspective, the legal reasoning takes into account beliefs and principles that are considered implemented in the legal system if we consider the open-texture context. The whole area of inherent-ambiguity reasoning seems to be lifted to a more abstract level: here we are not producing solutions to individual conflicts, but rules that are to guide all. We are no longer talking about Kazaa and El Cheapo, but about trends in areas of e-commerce more in general. If we focus, as we do, on e-commerce in cyberspace, we distinguish these areas by types of e-commerce (business-to-business, business-to-consumer and consumer-to-consumer) and by levels of services that support activities in cyberspace. These levels have been adopted from the framework Lessig[36] uses in his discussion of the way intellectual property law influences life on cyberspace. At the physical network level we find the physical resources whereon cyberspace exists, like copper, fibre and frequencies. At the code level we make a distinction between the areas of communication code (where the protocols and communication interfaces are) and application code (where application programs like word processors and Kazaa-clients and web servers are). At the content level, we find the knowledge and information, as provided and understood by businesses and consumers.

An interesting aspect of Table 4 is that it helps to show dependencies between industries. From a functional point of view, the content industry on cyberspace must make use of applications, communications and networks; the software industry must make use of communications and networks and the communication industry must make use of networks. The services on the lower levels are the infrastructures for the services at higher levels. In reverse, these infrastructure services are dependent on the demand from higher levels: when there is no interest in content, the infrastructure services remain idle. Consequently, the four layers of e-commercial services are sentenced to each

	B2B	B2C	C2C
Content			
Code: application			
Code: communication			
Physical networks			

Table 4: e-commerce areas

36 Lawrence Lessig, *The future of ideas* (Basic Books, 2001).

to which you owe the payment auto-draft the payment every month from the Monthly Fixed Account. Either way works. I do a little of both.

If you decide to have your bank pay the bill automatically, the bank generally has a relationship with the larger companies and can make that payment electronically. In this case, you can schedule the payment only a day or two before it's due and it will arrive on time. The software will generally ask you how you want to handle payments that fall on weekends and holidays, so take that into consideration. I generally have it pay 5 days in advance of the due date to cover weekends and/or holidays. For smaller companies or individuals that you want to pay automatically, the bank must send a check. Usually they tell you it can take 7 to 10 business days to arrive. This means you'll need to schedule those transactions a little further out to give the check time to arrive and give someone on the payment end time to post it. Don't worry though. All of this works flawlessly. Most banks provide these services free of charge. They even pay the postage to mail the check. If your bank charges for any of this, then it's probably time to get a new bank.

> **"All of this works flawlessly. Most banks provide these services free of charge."**

I want to be very clear about this, so let's try an example. Let's say your kids are in daycare. The daycare is small, maybe a local church or maybe even a stay-at-home mom that keeps a few kids. If the amount you pay for daycare is a fixed amount, you should pay it from the Monthly Fixed Account, and you should set it up where they get a check from your bank automatically every month at the same time. It doesn't matter if

> **"Schedule every fixed monthly expense to be paid automatically."**

Chapter 3

MONTHLY FIXED

Oh the Magic, No Debit Card

This account is such a beautiful thing. In my own budget, I actually call this account my "All The Good" account. Why? Because primarily in this account, I make my money do all the good things I want it to do, and it all happens automatically. Let's see how it works.

This account is for all your monthly expenses that are a fixed dollar amount. This includes things like your mortgage, car payment (get this out of your life, you don't need this stress), electric bill (I have mine set up on budget billing, so it is the same amount or very close every month), and maybe charitable contributions. Every single expense that occurs every month that is a fixed amount, or within a few dollars of being fixed, belongs in the Monthly Fixed Account. Maybe you have some credit card debt that you are determined to get rid of and you want to throw $500 a month at it until it's gone. I would put that here.

"Make your money do all the good things you want it to do, and make it all happen automatically."

Now let's assume that all your fixed monthly expenses add up to $2000. That means $2000 would transfer from the Holding Account to your Monthly Fixed Account either on the first of the month (ideally) or as you got paid. Since this expense amount is "fixed," you assign your bank to automatically transfer this same amount every single month from the Holding Account to the Monthly Fixed Account. Then you have your bank software pay each of those bills automatically and on time from the Monthly Fixed Account. Similarly, you could also have the companies

budget/expenses. We'll assume January is a good month and your income is $1200. So, $1200 goes into the Holding Account. However, since you only need $1000 to cover your expenses, only $1000 is automatically transferred out of the Holding Account and into the other accounts to cover your January expenses. The additional $200 that you didn't need in January just sits in the Holding Account waiting on the month that you are short. Let's say February your income is $800. So only $800 is deposited into the Holding Account. This is $200 short of the $1000 you need to meet your budget. Well, no worries, you have $200 left in the Holding Account from January. So again, on schedule $1000 is automatically transferred to the other accounts where it needs to go. Easy.

See what we just did there? Be honest, right now when that good month comes, you're spending it all that month and then when the bad months come, you're left scrambling. Maybe you're even using credit cards to make up the difference, but now those days are gone! You're getting better already and we've only just begun!

> **"You're getting better already, and we've only just begun!"**

Helpful Hint – *I do recommend having some "cushion" in the account wherever possible. Maybe that's $50 or $500...whatever you're comfortable with. I wouldn't take any account down to absolute $0 every month unless it was an absolute necessity. There could be a penalty associated with a $0 balance.*

Until you are able to save for a month's worth of expenses in the Holding Account and have it waiting for the upcoming month, the process would look like this. Let's say you are paid on the 1st and the 15th of the month. Both of those deposits should come directly into the Holding Account (direct deposit if possible). Then based off your situation and how you set it up, this money will immediately and automatically be disbursed to the other accounts as needed. Don't worry if you don't quite understand how it works yet. You will over the next couple of chapters. Remember you'll set all this money movement to happen automatically. After a few months, you won't even have to think about it.

Here's how you do it. Once all your accounts have been opened, I want you to access your online banking and tell it when, where, and how much money to transfer from the Holding Account to the other accounts. Literally, assign your bank's software the task of automatically moving a specific dollar amount on specific dates to specific accounts. In the example above of getting paid on the 1st and the 15th, I would likely have my bank disburse money out of my Holding Account to my other accounts on the 2nd and 16th. I know for some of you giving up that kind of control makes you a little queasy, but believe me, this is awesome. I have been doing this for years and I have never had even one mistake made by my bank's software. There have been mistakes, but when I research the mistakes, it was me!

> **"Literally, assign your bank's software the task of automatically moving a specific dollar amount on specific dates to specific accounts."**

Your situation might be such that your income isn't the same every month. In other words, some months you have plenty of money to cover expenses, but the next month your income doesn't quite cover expenses. This scenario actually works best within the system. Let's say you need $1000 every month to cover all your

Chapter 2

HOLDING ACCOUNT

No Debit Card

Let's start at the top. The Holding Account's job is to catch all your personal income streams and automatically distribute them to your other accounts as directed. All your salary or income streams should come into the Holding Account first, and this should happen via direct deposit if possible. The Holding Account can either be a checking or savings account. I generally have this as a savings account because there will be no debit card access to this account.

You might ask why it's important to have a Holding Account. Why can't you just allow your money to direct deposit into one of the other accounts and then disburse from there? Great question. The answer is simple. Eventually, I want you to have a month's salary or enough to cover a month's worth of expenses sitting in the Holding Account waiting until the 1st of the month before it disburses to the other accounts. I realize for many of you, that can't happen immediately, and that's okay. But, at some point, there's magic in transferring all the budget for the month from the Holding Account into the separate accounts on the 1st of the month. It makes everything much cleaner. Then while you're working through and living that month, all your income, whether you're paid weekly or bi-weekly, builds up in the Holding Account waiting for the first of the next month. Then, the process starts all over again. It's just a clean way to manage your monthly budget. Work hard toward this. You will thank me later.

> **"The Holding account catches all income streams and disburses them automatically."**

they're small or local or even an individual. Your bank can send them a check automatically as it would anyone else. Now, that's one less thing for you to worry about.

Remember how I said that having the money transfer on the 1st day of the month (or 2nd) is ideal? Let's discuss the ideal 1st day of the month transfer first. Let's go into your online banking and set up an automatic transfer of $2000 to occur on the 1st day of every month from the Holding Account to the Monthly Fixed Account with no end date. This means that from now on, $2000 will transfer automatically, and if your expenses never change, then you'll never have to worry about it again. Of course, things will change over time but not as much or as often as you might think. When things do change, simply go in and change the dollar amount. Done!

Now how does this work if you're paid every two weeks? This just takes a little more strategy and planning. Let's use that $2000 expense number again, and let's say you don't have the reserves yet to hold a whole month's salary in the Holding Account waiting for the first of the month. In other words, when you get paid, you must put that money to work immediately. That's okay. You'll get there. Let's assume you get paid every two weeks. Let's assume your mortgage of $1000 is due on the 10th and your other expenses equaling $1000 are due on the 25th. In this example, your paychecks would still go into the Holding Account. The amount needed on the 10th would be set to automatically transfer into the Monthly Fixed Account in time to pay the mortgage. Also, remember that the mortgage is set up to be paid automatically. In this example, since the other bills aren't due until the 25th, money will sit in the Holding Account until it's time to pay the bills due on the 25th. Again, this transfer is automatic and the bills are paid automatically.

> **“Regardless of how often you get paid, this system still works.”**

Whew! I know that was a lot to take in, so let's quickly review so you don't get discouraged or lose focus. In its simplest form, remember this is all that's happening. You have fixed expenses every month, or expenses that do not regularly change. These expenses include things like your mortgage and maybe car payments. You will set up the Monthly Fixed Account to pay those expenses automatically. This means you no longer worry about whether you've paid the most important expenses you have every month.

You may not believe this, but my mortgage payment never crosses my mind. My Monthly Fixed Account pays that mortgage on time every month. Here's a bonus. Vanessa and I decided years ago to pay extra on the mortgage. We have built that extra into our monthly fixed payment.

This means I don't have to make the decision every month to pay extra on my mortgage. I've committed to pay my mortgage off early, and I'm actually doing it, without thinking about it. Bam! Trust me. You're gonna love this.

Helpful Hint *– Remember if you currently have monthly fixed bills auto-drafted from any of your other bank accounts, you will want to re- direct those to this account.*

Chapter 4

IRREGULAR EXPENSES

Maybe debit card, you decide

The Irregular Expenses Account is a holding place for expenses that we know are going to occur but they either don't occur monthly or the amount isn't fixed.

This account is going to give you so many wonderful moments of, "Oh no, the alternator went out on the car! Wait, we've been putting money aside for that every month. Ok cool, fix the car. No worries!"

> **"OK cool, fix the car. No worries!"**

That is exactly how I feel and react every single time, even to this day, when an unplanned but inevitable expense occurs. You may ask, "If it's unplanned, doesn't that make it an emergency?" No. We know these things are going to happen, we just don't know the date and time. It's like keeping an umbrella in your car. We know eventually rain is coming. We don't know the very moment it will start, but we plan for it by keeping an umbrella handy. When will the brakes go out on your car? When will the tires wear out? When might an alternator go out? We don't have a fixed date for these expenses. We really don't have a fixed dollar amount for these expenses, so how in the world do we plan for them? First things first. We know these things are going to happen. We know cars break down, and brakes wear out. So if we know these things are going to happen, we need a plan for them. However, we don't need to have some major algebraic equation and an actuarial chart to create a strategy.

What are some other things that might fit into the Irregular Expenses Account? How about events we know are coming like birthdays, Christmas, graduation, etc. Listen, you know you're going to get those kids something for Christmas this year—you are. So why are we surprised when we wake up the Friday after Thanksgiving and say, "HOLY SMOKES! Christmas is just around the corner! How are we going to buy gifts?" Christmas is the same time every single year. We can do better than this. Here's how.

The way I manage this account is simple to understand but takes a little time to prepare.

Here is a list of some irregular expenses that are common:

- Birthdays
- Anniversaries
- Medical Expenses
- Dental Expenses
- Auto Repair
- Christmas
- Car Insurance (if it's not monthly fixed)
- Home Repair
- School clothes for kids
- Kid's sports or activity dues
- Vacation/Travel

Now I want you to create a list like I did above of things you have paid for over the last 12 months **<u>excluding</u>** monthly fixed expenses. Also **<u>exclude</u>** normal living expenses like food or gas.

Second, go to your handy dandy computer and print off every bank statement or credit card statement from the last 12 months. It doesn't matter if you do a calendar year (Jan - Dec) or if you start with your current month and look back 12 months.

Now take a highlighter and highlight anything that you feel falls within the list that you made. Don't worry about keeping them separated. We are going to pay these out of one account. Now that you've highlighted them–add them all up. This number may shock you a little and can be a little scary. I'll bet you had no idea you paid that much for those kinds of things! Now let's do a little division. Take that big number and divide it by 12. Let's say that number equaled $3600. If we divide that by 12 we get $300. This means that every month, you will have the Holding Account transfer $300 into the Irregular Expenses Account. When one of the above things occur, you won't have to worry about it. Take your checkbook for this account or debit card and just pay it.

> **"When one of the above things occur, you won't have to worry about it."**

Helpful hint. – *Since you're going to have multiple debit cards in your wallet/purse, make sure you write the name of each account on your debit card for you and your partner.*

If having debit card access to this money is too tempting, restrict access to this account. Choose not to have a debit card. How would that work? When an expense comes up that falls into the Irregular Expenses Account category, determine how much you'll need to cover the expense, then transfer just that amount from the Irregular Expenses Account into your Everyday Expenses Account (next chapter). Then use your Everyday Expenses Account debit card. This puts a step between you and a bad spur-of-the-moment spending decision with your Irregular Expenses dollars. It forces you to go into your account and transfer the money. That gives you time to think before you just whip out the debit card and pay for something you don't need.

This Irregular Expenses Account will always be a work in progress. You will never get it exactly right down to the dollar. In the beginning, you could put $300 in there the first month then have a $500 car repair. That's okay. That's life. Once you get it going, things will normalize over time. If you end a calendar year with too much money in this account, then adjust and fund a little less

> **"The Irregular Expenses Account will always be a work in progress."**

the next year. What if you run out of money in this account? You'll need to invest a few more dollars in there every month.

So how do you manage if your car repair and home repair are more this year than they were last year? Great question! It could be that the gifts we give this year aren't as expensive. Maybe we will have to work a little overtime. We might even have to pull a little from the Everyday Expenses Account that we'll discuss next. The important thing is that you assign a reasonable dollar amount to go into this account every single month. Why? Because we know these expenses are coming, and we don't want to put them on a credit card or borrow money from parents or somewhere else.

"We know these expenses are coming and we don't want to put them on a credit card or borrow money from parents or somewhere else."

This account will create tremendous peace in your life. You can do this!

Chapter 5

EVERYDAY EXPENSES

Has Debit Card

That gets us to the Everyday Expenses Account. This account is where the Holding Account will transfer most of what's left from your salaries after you've funded the Monthly Fixed and Irregular Expenses Accounts. The Everyday Expenses Account is for your day to day living expenses.

Before we move on, let's make sure to make a mental note of where you are in simple terms. We have already automatically made our money do everything it was supposed to do! What does that mean? It means we have set up our Monthly Fixed Account and our Irregular Expenses Account to handle the big financial obligations in our life. It means we are financially awesome, and we are being great stewards of what God has given us. We're not flying by the seat of our pants any longer. We have a plan. Sure, it's a plan that basically runs itself. Sure, it feels like doing good ought to be harder than this, but it's not! This means our remaining dollars are to some degree discretionary. How does that feel? Good, right?

"It feels like doing good ought to be harder than this, but it's not!"

I know, I know. You haven't eaten yet, you haven't put any gas in the car, and you haven't purchased clothes. But everyone has some discretion over those decisions. For example, if your income is a little lower this month, don't eat out–eat sandwiches. You can also choose not to drive unless it's absolutely necessary. You can make the decision to keep wearing your old clothes for a while longer (these clothes aren't old; they're vintage), or you can buy the clothes you must have from the thrift store. That's right! It won't kill you. I promise. The bottom line is everyone has choices in areas like these.

With that being said, all that is left to do is manage the amount of money in the Everyday Expenses Account. This is easily done by dividing the money in this account by the number of days left in the month. For example, if there are 10 days left in the month and only $200 left in this account, quick math will tell you, you can only average spending $20 per day for the rest of the month. It's that easy! You don't need fancy budgeting, spreadsheets, or software. Simply look at the total dollars in this account and manage your spending with your mind. This account is where I'd heavily recommend bank account visibility on your mobile phone. You need to know how much is in this account at all times.

"You don't need fancy budgeting, spreadsheets, or software."

Think that's too much temptation? Well then, do it this way. Let's say you've determined that $800 is going to go into this account every month. For easy math, let's go with a 4-week month. You could have your Holding Account transfer $200 at the beginning of each week into the Everyday Expenses Account automatically. This will prevent you from spending the entire budget for this account in the first week. Look at you. You're budgeting without even trying!

"Look at you, you're budgeting without even trying!"

In our household, we transfer the entire amount on the first day of the month and we just manage the dollars as the month progresses. Some months, we'll spend too much in week one, and that means we must be more careful in weeks two through four. If we're not careful, we may run out of money. But remember, even if you spend too much in week one, guess what? You haven't risked your house payment or car payment. You're only working with money that has very little risk attached to it. In most of American households, I'd be willing to bet that if you couldn't buy food for one week, you wouldn't starve. There are enough cans of beans and Ramen noodles and tuna in the pantry, not to mention the food in the freezer you haven't looked at in two years.

The bottom line is that you will learn to manage these dollars and work it out week by week. Even in our household, by the fourth week, we're definitely ready to get paid again. We run this account low every single month. Should feel bad about that? No! I've already done all the good I wanted to do in my other accounts. There is no condemnation and nothing to feel guilty about.

How does it feel to be free? Amazing!

Helpful Hint – *Don't forget to label your debit cards.*

Chapter 6

HIS/HER FREEDOM

Debit Card or Cash

You've made it! All the hard work is over. You have made it to fun time! Everybody needs a little money to blow. Men, women, kids, and old financial misers like myself need a little bit of money to spend however we want with no guilt and no judgement. The Freedom Accounts make this a priority. For some of you, these may not even be accounts yet. You may just pull this amount in cash, but the important thing is to have some dollars individually that each partner has complete control over.

Here is my real-world example. After setting up all of our accounts, my lovely wife Vanessa and I decided together how much to put into her Freedom Account each month. Those dollars are her dollars. I no longer have any say whatsoever over how she spends those. She can save them over several months and buy something big, or she can spend every penny every month. She can buy shoes and more shoes. She can literally roll the car window down and toss those dollars out of the window. Are you ready to hear what my response is going to be no matter what she does with the money? My job is to be her cheerleader! "Wow, Babe! Nobody throws money out the window as well as you do! You are amazing!" Obviously, that scenario is ridiculous, but it does make my point. There is nothing she can do with that money that I don't applaud. It's hers to enjoy. Likewise, the money in my Freedom Account is the same. I challenge any of you who know our family to ask my wife if I have ever questioned, even one time, what she has spent. She will smile and tell you I have not. She loves it.

> **"There is nothing she can do with that money that I don't applaud."**

Here's another way you can modify this whole plan. Vanessa does the grocery shopping in our household. After looking back at what we've spent in the past on groceries, we determined a monthly dollar amount for that. We decided to add that amount to her Freedom Account. Why? Because if she can use coupons or figure out a way to make that money go further, she has more money in her Freedom Account to spend. Do I recommend this for everyone? No. This customization requires great trust, built through years of good habits, earned by both parties. This is just the way we do it and an example of how to make this program work for your family. What happens if we're having a lot of people over to our house for dinner and that event is going to seriously eat into her monthly amount. We talk about it and figure out how to manage that event separately. We don't lock ourselves down and become slaves to the program. The program is meant to free you, not enslave you or beat you down. This program should never be the stick we use to beat each other up with when there's a mistake or hiccup. We figure out how to move on, and we do better next time.

"This program should never be the stick we use to beat each other up with when there's a mistake or hiccup."

Chapter 7

THE HOW TO

The Nuts & Bolts

Opening Accounts

The nuts and bolts of setting up these accounts at your bank will not be the same as mine. My bank is not a large international bank; it's a regional bank. All the technology I need to run the system is readily available. I set up my accounts online. If you're wanting to set all of this up at a new bank you've never had an account with before, it will likely require a visit to that bank. Before you try to open the accounts, I recommend sitting down and deciding exactly how many accounts you want to open, and what the mix is going to be of savings accounts and checking accounts. Then get started online, on the phone, or in person. For some of you, in person is going to be easier. My bank calls my checking accounts "freebie checking." This means there are no rewards points, no frills, and low interest rates. These accounts are just basic accounts with debit cards and electronic access. Electronic access means I can view the account online, make changes, make deposits, pay bills, etc., and do it all from my computer or smart phone.

> **"The technology needed to run this system is readily avaialable."**

Another feature my bank offers, which I'm sure yours will too, is the ability to assign each account a name or nickname, – whatever you want. This way when you are looking at your accounts online, the account names will match what you're calling them at home.

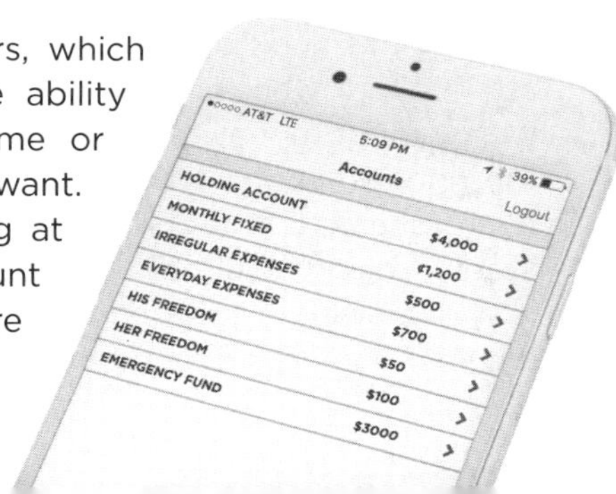

I believe this is important. Remember to write the name on the back of the debit card associated with each account. I write it with a sharpie and then put a piece of tape over it so it doesn't smudge or wear off.

Can I Do This In Stages?

Yes! You may want to do this in stages. Start with your Holding Account, Monthly Fixed Account, and Everyday Expenses Account. Determine what your monthly fixed expenses are and set up the Holding Account to transfer those dollars into the Monthly Fixed Account. Then, have all other dollars go to the Everyday Expenses Account. That way you're getting accustomed to the automation before you jump in all the way.

Setting Up Automatic Transactions

Remember, the "automatic" piece of this system is where the magic lives. Just having a bunch of accounts open can help organize some things, but what makes this system is having your money moving around and paying bills automatically.

I generally work in two areas within my bank's software. They are Fund Transfers and Bill Pay.

Fund Transfer

This tool allows you to automatically set up monthly or weekly transfers between accounts. This is the tool you will use to automatically move money from the Holding Account to all other accounts as you've determined with your partner after reading this book and discussing. It is important to pay real close attention to when and where you're moving the money. Don't worry about money getting lost. Just make sure you are moving the right amount of money to the right place at the right time. It's not hard to fix a mistake. However, when you're getting this system rolling, you may have a bill that doesn't get paid, or you may overdraft an account if you're not careful. There shouldn't be any fear here. Just pay attention, and don't get distracted during the first month or two.

Bill Pay

This tool in your bank's software will help you schedule your Monthly Fixed Account to pay your monthly fixed bills that aren't being auto-drafted. When setting this up, you are going to need information about the company/individual that will be receiving this payment. So it's a good idea to have the bill in front of you.

Chapter 8

EMERGENCY FUND

No Debit Card

This is a savings account and this account is critical to your financial success! Life happens, and at some point, something completely unexpected and impossible to plan for is going to occur. That's why we have the Emergency Fund.

It's important to have access, but not easy access to this money. I would recommend you open this account in another bank. Set up this account so that you have limited access. You may want to consider setting it up so that you have to physically go to the bank to get this money if you need it. Why? Because if it's too easy to get to, then it's too easy to get to. Most of us will lie to ourselves and say, "I'll borrow a little from the Emergency Fund this month, and I'll pay it back next month." My friends that never works! So, put an obstacle between you and these dollars.

What constitutes an "emergency?" An emergency is job loss, or perhaps the hot water heater explodes in your house, and you need to pay someone immediately to clean up the mess before the insurance company can get you a check. These are emergencies. Things like kids braces, tires, brakes, and gifts are not emergencies. Why? Because we already know these things are coming. Forgetting your sister's birthday yesterday isn't an emergency. It's been the same day since she was born. We have been planning for these events in your other accounts. These events are important. They're just not emergencies.

> **"What constitutes an "emergency?""**

You may be wondering, "How much should I have in my Emergency Fund?" Great question. Most experts agree that savings equal to 3–6 months of expenses should be enough. Don't panic if that seems like an impossibility to you. Let's start small. Make a goal to put $500 into your Emergency Fund as quickly as possible. Make some sacrifices, or have a yard sale. Just do whatever you can to put that buffer between you and life. Try to never spend that money. Work hard to build it up to the target amount of 3-6 months worth of expenses. You can do this. Nothing worth doing is ever going to be easy. All worthwhile endeavors are uphill. This is not too big for you. Ain't nothin but a step for a stepper!

"How much should I have in my Emergency Fund?"

Chapter 9

SAVING FOR THE FUTURE

Now It's Getting Fun

I don't give this account a certain name because this type of savings can come in many forms. Here's the bottom line, one day you will retire and slow down. Maybe you're forced to retire due to poor health or an accident. Maybe at some point you just want to do something else like volunteer, spend time with family, and/or travel, without worrying about having to make more money.

"One day you will retire or slow down."

Talk to your accountant about the best tax favored vehicle for you. Find a Certified Financial Planner who works on a fee-only basis and under fiduciary guidelines-not your insurance salesman. I don't want you talking to someone who is working off of a commission for retirement saving advice. I want someone who gets paid a fixed percentage (like 1%) of your total invested assets. Since that's how they are paid, their incentive is to help you grow that account.

I love IRAs, Roth IRAs, 401ks, Roth 401ks, and 403bs. Any of these types of accounts may be a good fit for you. I especially like any retirement vehicle that your employer is matching. Just remember that like the other accounts, this needs to be funded automatically. When do you start? Now! When is the best time to plant a tree? Twenty years ago. When is the second best time? Now! Time is a major factor in growing your wealth. Start early, and teach your kids to start early.

Then what do you invest in? I personally like passive or index investing. However, all of that is for another book and another time. Just start saving for the future; it'll be here before you know it.

Chapter 10

THE WRAP UP

You Can Do This!

People who do well with their money don't do well by accident. You must do something. You must make something happen. Yes, doing a written budget every month is the very best way to manage your money. However, if you can't or won't stick with a budget–it's worthless. You need to find a money management system you can or will do. I believe this plan to automate all your financial transactions is the second best way to manage your money. It can become the very best way-only if you use it.

> **"People who do well with their money don't do well by accident."**

I'm proud of you for reading this book. What this tells me is that you're a person who is serious about taking control of your finances. You are so much further ahead than almost everyone around you. Don't stop here. Push. If you're single, go for it! If you're married, get your partner to join you, and work together to change your family's future. Teach others.

You've got this!

Notes

Notes